CAR..

Caryl Churchill has written for the stage, television and radio. Her stage plays include *Owners* (Royal Court Theatre Upstairs, 1972); *Objections to Sex and Violence* (Royal Court, 1975); *Light Shining in Buckinghamshire* (Joint Stock on tour incl. Theatre Upstairs, 1976); *Vinegar Tom* (Monstrous Regiment on tour, incl. Half Moon and ICA, 1976); *Traps* (Theatre Upstairs, 1977), *Cloud Nine* (Joint Stock on tour incl. Royal Court, London, 1979, then Theatre de Lys, New York, 1981); *Three More Sleepless Nights* (Soho Poly and Theatre Upstairs, 1980); *Top Girls* (Royal Court, London, then Public Theater, New York, 1982); *Fen* (Joint Stock on tour, incl. Almeida and Royal Court, London, then Public Theater, New York, 1983); *Softcops* (RSC at the Pit, 1984); *A Mouthful of Birds* with David Lan (Joint Stock on tour, incl. Royal Court, 1986); *Serious Money* (Royal Court and Wyndham's, London, then Public Theater, New York, 1987); *Icecream* (Royal Court, 1989); *Mad Forest* (Central School of Speech and Drama, then Royal Court, 1990); *Lives of the Great Poisoners* with Orlando Gough and Ian Spink (Second Stride on tour, incl. Riverside Studios, London, 1991); *The Skriker* (Royal National Theatre, 1994); *Thyestes* translated from Seneca (Royal Court Theatre Upstairs, 1994); *Hotel* with Orlando Gough and Ian Spink (Second Stride on tour, incl. The Place, London, 1997); *This is a Chair* (London International Festival of Theatre at the Royal Court, 1997); *Blue Heart* (Joint Stock on tour, incl. Royal Court Theatre, 1997); *Far Away* (Royal Court Theatre Upstairs, 2000, and Albery, London, 2001, then New York Theatre Workshop, 2002); *A Number* (Royal Court Theatre, 2002 and the New York Theatre Workshop, 2004).

Plays by Caryl Churchill published by TCG

Blue Heart

Cloud 9

A Dream Play
(adapted from August Strindberg)

Far Away

Light Shining in Buckinghamshire

Mad Forest

A Number

The Skriker

This is a Chair

DRUNK ENOUGH
TO SAY I LOVE YOU?

Caryl Churchill

THEATRE COMMUNICATIONS GROUP

NEW YORK

2008

A CIP catalog record for this book is available from the Library of Congress

TCG books are exclusively distributed to the book trade by Consortium Book Sales and Distribution.

Cover design by Lisa Govan

First TCG Edition, March 2008

Drunk Enough to Say I Love You? was first performed at the Royal Court Jerwood Theatre Downstairs, London, on 10 November 2006, with the following cast:

SAM   Ty Burrell
JACK   Stephen Dillane

Director James Macdonald
Designer Eugene Lee
Costume Designer Joan Wadge
Lighting Designer Peter Mumford
Sound Designer Ian Dickinson
Composer Matthew Herbert

The production received its American premiere at The Public Theater, New York, on 5 March 2008, with the following cast:

SAM   Scott Cohen
GUY   Samuel West

Note

Sam was always called Sam, because of Uncle Sam. I gave the other character the name Jack, thinking of it as just a name, but some people understandably thought it referred to Union Jack, and that Jack was Britain in the same way that Sam was America. But I always meant that character to be an individual, a man who falls in love with America, so I have changed his name to Guy.

C.C.

DRUNK ENOUGH
TO SAY I LOVE YOU?

Characters

SAM, *a country*

GUY, *a man*

1.

GUY	drunk enough to say I love you?
SAM	never say
GUY	not that I don't still love my wife and children but
SAM	who doesn't want to be loved? but
GUY	first time I saw you
SAM	the bar and the guy with
GUY	never see you again and I was fine with that, I thought one night and I'll love him till I die but that's ok, I can live
SAM	you know something?
GUY	and then I'm here and suddenly here you are and here we are again and
SAM	because I'm leaving tomorrow so
GUY	sorry of course but just as well because
SAM	and you could come with me if you
GUY	I
SAM	if you want
GUY	of course I

SAM	so you'll
GUY	so no I can't possibly
SAM	of course not
GUY	no
SAM	glad you came over and said hi because when you reminded me it all came back though to be honest I'd forgotten till you
GUY	can't say no oh god can't let you
SAM	so you'll
GUY	what I'm going to tell them. How long
SAM	as long as it
GUY	family obviously but work, I'm in the middle
SAM	sure you'll figure it out, I don't need to
GUY	go where did you say you?
SAM	anywhere you wouldn't?
GUY	do when we get there?
SAM	things you won't do?

2.

GUY	music, I can't get enough of
SAM	country or
GUY	when I listen to Bessie Smith or
SAM	Dylan, Bing Crosby, Eminem
GUY	because what rock does
SAM	even Jingle Bells can suddenly
GUY	the snow and all the
SAM	mountains like you've never
GUY	size of it all, there's so many different
SAM	sea to shining
GUY	freedom to
SAM	Ellis Island
GUY	or even just go to the movies and eat popcorn
SAM	pursuit of happiness
GUY	right now
SAM	how to keep
GUY	because it's so
SAM	elections

GUY	how to win
SAM	because democracy
GUY	help the right side to
SAM	because our security
GUY	all over the world
SAM	Vietnam we have the slogan 'Christ has gone south' so the people think
GUY	Christians because of the French
SAM	literally believe literally Jesus Christ has
GUY	so clever
SAM	and simultaneously astrology
GUY	superstitious
SAM	horoscopes daily horoscopes will say
GUY	and they vote the way you want, that is so
SAM	because you have to appeal to their deepest
GUY	I love this
SAM	and Chile, this is good, we put it on the radio 'your children taken from you', if they vote communist they lose their children, the Russians will take
GUY	appealing to the women's vote
SAM	so the pamphlets must say 'privately printed by citizens with no political affiliations' because

GUY	big budget
SAM	and syndicate the articles all over the world
GUY	so nobody
SAM	and posters
GUY	great artwork
SAM	with the hammer and sickle stamped on their foreheads
GUY	little kids
SAM	hammer and sickle
GUY	love a copy of that to put
SAM	So help me out here, in Nicaragua we need to be telling different things to different groups, say
GUY	fighting to keep the Russians off their land because peasants
SAM	while the workers
GUY	that they'll lose their factories
SAM	doctors
GUY	replaced by Cubans
SAM	way to go.
GUY	so happy, you, the work, the whole
SAM	polls in the Phillipines?
GUY	so I'll make the numbers up

SAM	good at this
GUY	thrilling.
SAM	don't always work out the way we
GUY	voting for the wrong
SAM	Chavez
GUY	how did
SAM	Hamas
GUY	Israelis arresting the Members of Parliament so
SAM	so now we need to prevent some elections
GUY	saves having to overthrow
SAM	South Korea, Guatemala, Brazil, Congo, Indonesia, Greece
GUY	I'm on it
SAM	overthrow only as last resort when things don't
GUY	ok
SAM	Iran Guatemala Iraq Congo
GUY	troops
SAM	coffee
GUY	two sugars
SAM	invading Grenada to get rid of the government because

GUY	byebye Lumumba
SAM	byebye Allende
GUY	bit negative
SAM	people we love and help
GUY	Israel
SAM	shah of Iran, byebye Mossadegh
GUY	oil
SAM	Saddam Hussein
GUY	great
SAM	shake his hand
GUY	holding down the ayatollahs
SAM	warlords in Afghanistan, Hekmatya
GUY	drives over people?
SAM	acid
GUY	ok
SAM	don't like that government in Afghanistan because the Russians like it so we're tricking them into invading
GUY	oops
SAM	puts them in the wrong plus it's their Vietnam so now get on with training the mujahadeen which is freedom fighters to
GUY	whooo

SAM	haha
GUY	so we're helping all these
SAM	kind of want to help Pol Pot because
GUY	killing fields guy?
SAM	against Vietnam but no we can't be seen to directly support someone who
GUY	so why don't we help China help him
SAM	knew I was right to bring you
GUY	because no one can blame us for what the Chinese
SAM	and all costs money
GUY	so much aid
SAM	and two hundred and fifty million dollars to the Phillipines alone to train fifty thousand soldiers
GUY	plus military advisers
SAM	remember to use Green Berets of Puerto Rican and Mexican descent so it won't look like a US army because
GUY	ha
SAM	would you believe six billion dollars in El Salvador? training thousands of
GUY	and the schools, I'm trying to organise
SAM	School of the Americas
GUY	coup school

SAM	Chemical School
GUY	enormous.
SAM	results in and we won in
GUY	yay
SAM	and we've got our man in Afghanistan
GUY	CIA guy?
SAM	Georgia check
GUY	Uzbekistan? because they boil
SAM	not so good in Bolivia
GUY	guy in the sweater?
SAM	and Saddam's let us down, he's no longer a good guy so
GUY	because sometimes propaganda isn't enough to
SAM	military solution
GUY	so much fun in my life
SAM	being powerful and being on the side of good is
GUY	God must have so much fun
SAM	win win win
GUY	love you more than I can

3.

SAM	sitting around
GUY	not
SAM	so much to do because
GUY	thinking
SAM	no time for
GUY	all right I'm just
SAM	missing your
GUY	not at all
SAM	natural
GUY	get on with
SAM	because there's all these people we have to
GUY	ok so here's the bridge right here and the people there are people going across not soldiers just
SAM	North Korea
GUY	blow it up
SAM	there you go
GUY	don't want you to worry because I don't regret

SAM	death squads
GUY	right behind
SAM	in Guatemala, so we don't directly ourselves appear to
GUY	corpses in the nets
SAM	decapitated, castrated, eyes gouged out, testicles
GUY	riddled with bullets and partially eaten by fish
SAM	slaughter the Indians to prevent
GUY	bulldoze the village
SAM	yes
GUY	and
SAM	not officially active in El Salvador
GUY	seventy-five thousand civilian
SAM	raping the
GUY	because if the young aren't killed they just grow up to be
SAM	similarly Colombia where
GUY	Nicaragua
SAM	our freedom fighters the Contras are
GUY	Indonesia the embassy's giving lists to their army which are a big help in who they should

SAM	mass slaying
GUY	there you are
SAM	and of course Israel where we don't actually ourselves
GUY	extremely valuable experiment in the Philippines where
SAM	calling it search and destroy
GUY	experiments in pacification
SAM	terror against the Huks
GUY	and applying that now in Vietnam
SAM	Vietnam Vietnam now
GUY	go go go three million dead in Vietnam Laos Cambodia
SAM	two million tons of bombs on Laos now
GUY	more than on Germany and Japan in the whole
SAM	white phosphorous
GUY	statistics here on civilian injuries, lower extremities 60%, soft tissue 39%, fractures
SAM	not that interested
GUY	Iraq
SAM	not that interested in numbers of civilian
GUY	no
SAM	need to get on

GUY	I'm on it
SAM	Iraq
GUY	hundred and seventy-seven million pounds of
SAM	forty days
GUY	ten thousand sorties
SAM	very few casualties
GUY	oh ours, good
SAM	bombing them now as they retreat
GUY	ploughing wow ploughing live soldiers into the sand
SAM	done
GUY	and the children dead from sanctions we don't count that because
SAM	again Iraq Iraq again
GUY	very few casualties
SAM	not publishing pictures
GUY	and certainly not of the civilians in Afghanistan there's a paper in Florida making a mistake there getting a lot of emails and won't do that again
SAM	bombing Vietnam now, bombing Grenada, bombing Korea, bombing Laos, bombing Guatemala, bombing Cuba, bombing El Salvador, bombing Iraq, bombing Somalia, bombing Lebanon

GUY	but it's Israel bombing
SAM	so? bombing Bosnia, bombing Cambodia, bombing Libya, bombing
GUY	used to be a village and now
SAM	because we want it gone
GUY	need a coffee
SAM	get a coffee
GUY	exhausting
SAM	thrilling
GUY	exhausting being so thrilled
SAM	coffee but keep
GUY	bombing China, bombing Panama
SAM	good at this
GUY	well
SAM	did a whole lot before like second world war and going right back
GUY	all the back killings before like Indians
SAM	never sure how many we started
GUY	maybe twenty million, fifty
SAM	got them down to a quarter million so
GUY	not looking at that
SAM	no just get on with the job which is bombing
GUY	bombing Peru, bombing

4.

GUY	controlling
SAM	not
GUY	I feel
SAM	missing your family
GUY	only human, I'm naturally going to
SAM	just so I know where I am
GUY	expect me to just cut off everybody and not even speak
SAM	what you want
GUY	better if I do some
SAM	drawing up trade agreements
GUY	free trade
SAM	in a manner of
GUY	free
SAM	Structural Adjustment Programs
GUY	so that countries open up their markets to our
SAM	good ok like Haiti
GUY	surge in our rice exports to Haiti

SAM   ok

GUY   stopping the banana cartel

SAM   ok

GUY   and those beautiful African textiles made
           from our raw materials they agree to
           import rather than

SAM   or sometimes it's the other way, it's their
           raw materials like cocoa

GUY   and we make the chocolates you get on
           Valentine's

SAM   because if they were allowed to make
           them

GUY   and the rice industry collapses in Haiti

SAM   because our economy is the priority here

GUY   costing poor countries two billion dollars a

SAM   really snitty mood today

GUY   just trying to understand exactly

SAM   essential because we consume more than
           half the goods in the world so you can't

GUY   ok ok and privatisation a condition

SAM   because private means free

GUY   ok

SAM   problem with that?

GUY   just low today, I can't quite

SAM	better get a grip
GUY	ok so it's access for our goods
SAM	come on we've done debt cancellation here
GUY	yes I
SAM	and massive aid
GUY	linked to
SAM	what is the matter with you?
GUY	pointing out that it's 80% our own companies that benefit from
SAM	generosity
GUY	point one percent of our
SAM	billions of dollars for christsake
GUY	just trying to see
SAM	yes and
GUY	Israel seems to get the largest share of
SAM	you want to go home?
GUY	didn't say
SAM	because if you don't want to be
GUY	I do
SAM	keep saying you love me and then we have all this
GUY	sorry

SAM   easy to

GUY   woke up feeling

SAM   maybe you should go back to bed and try
                again

GUY   no I'll be

SAM   you better be

GUY   ok.

SAM   something to make you feel better

GUY   don't really

SAM   good?

GUY   ah

SAM   french connection

GUY   mm?

SAM   golden triangle

GUY   sure

SAM   fighting Communists for us so we turn a
                blind eye

GUY   of course

SAM   heroin being flown in by Air America

GUY   excellent

SAM   flying down with the weapons and back
                with the drugs

GUY   shrimp company laundering the money so
                the CIA

SAM	22 tons of cocaine though he himself is head of the antidrug
GUY	but also we are against
SAM	totally
GUY	like in Peru
SAM	supporting the dictator because he's fighting drugs
GUY	though I see here the CIA payroll
SAM	because the main priority is suppressing the guerrillas
GUY	like in Colombia
SAM	because FARC are definitely narcotraffickers
GUY	luckily
SAM	have to overlook the security services drug
GUY	and the equipment can also be used against trade unionists which saves
SAM	but in Afghanistan where of course the mujahadeen
GUY	beautiful fields of poppies
SAM	same trucks can deliver the arms and take the heroin back
GUY	so sometimes crack down and
SAM	massive trade figures

GUY   lot of people happy.

SAM   feeling better have a look at intellectual
             property rights

GUY   fascinating

SAM   forefront of science

GUY   traditional knowledge of primitive tribes
             which turns out to

SAM   neem

GUY   is what, neem?

SAM   in India

GUY   so we patent it do we and

SAM   ayehuasca, you ever heard ?

GUY   quinoa, kava, bitter gourd

SAM   so we're manufacturing products out of

GUY   and selling them back to

SAM   yes

GUY   and most amazingly DNA

SAM   Amazonian Indian blood cells

GUY   the scale of it

SAM   per cent of human DNA has been
             acquired by

GUY   my god how

SAM   so you're on that?

GUY	I'm on it.
SAM	because expenses are so huge like eight billion dollars we spend on cosmetics
GUY	hard to grasp such
SAM	ten on petfood
GUY	for comparison
SAM	six on
GUY	enough to provide health, food and education for the whole of the third
SAM	fuck is wrong with you?
GUY	trying to grasp the numbers that's all, I
SAM	do things on a large scale
GUY	yes
SAM	way of life
GUY	yes
SAM	you chose
GUY	yes
SAM	can fuck off now if
GUY	no
SAM	yes fuck off now because
GUY	no please no
SAM	commitment

24

5.

SAM	space
GUY	god
SAM	all mine
GUY	so
SAM	deny others the use of space
GUY	it's just
SAM	we have it, we like it and we're going to keep it
GUY	fantastic
SAM	fight *in* space, we're going to fight *from* space, we're going to fight *into*
GUY	wow
SAM	you like it?
GUY	so big
SAM	star wars
GUY	and protect
SAM	protecting us with a shield
GUY	and nobody else can
SAM	precision strikes

GUY	though the UN
SAM	everyone else agrees a resolution not to use space so
GUY	giving us total
SAM	because with the proliferation of WMD
GUY	so many countries want
SAM	so we combat the threat by
GUY	I do worry about
SAM	because we have two and a half times the next nine countries put together
GUY	thank god
SAM	nuclear weapons stored in seven European
GUY	hey
SAM	chemical
GUY	whoo
SAM	go go go now dioxin
GUY	dioxin, god, three ounces in the water supply of New York would be enough to wipe out the whole
SAM	five hundred pounds dioxin now on Vietnam
GUY	yay
SAM	napalm
GUY	yay

SAM   sarin on Laos

GUY   yay

SAM   and biological too the most advanced

GUY   scientific

SAM   turkey feathers

GUY   feathers?

SAM   allegations by China that we

GUY   oh with germs on

SAM   decaying fish, anthrax

GUY   isn't it turkey in Cuba?

SAM   turkey virus in Cuba

GUY   ok

SAM   contaminate the sugar

GUY   quite funny

SAM   but the serious science

GUY   the Chemical School in Alabama

SAM   teach our allies and share

GUY   Egypt's using gas against the Yemen, and
             Saddam's gassing the

SAM   exporting anthrax to Iraq, botulism,
             histoplasma capsulatum

GUY   e coli?

SAM   e coli, DNA

GUY	this stuff against Kurds or Iranians or?
SAM	keep selling it because
GUY	so great about chemical and biological they don't destroy the buildings just kill the
SAM	ideal
GUY	and oh my god the conventional
SAM	cluster bombs
GUY	love the yellow
SAM	jagged steel shrapnel
GUY	soft targets
SAM	don't always explode like one and a half million unexploded in the gulf
GUY	very high rate of
SAM	no, out of thirty
GUY	ok
SAM	but sometimes a quarter
GUY	orange groves, car parks
SAM	so don't let Israel
GUY	ok
SAM	oh what the hell
GUY	ok
SAM	so you get these accidental
GUY	kids like the yellow

SAM	accidental loss of limbs
GUY	can't be helped
SAM	and the depleted uranium so you get the lung and bone cancer and
GUY	don't feel bad
SAM	babies, deformed
GUY	ugh
SAM	probably for other reasons
GUY	exactly
SAM	So, keeping ourselves safe
GUY	priority
SAM	bring freedom
GUY	love it when you say
SAM	most destructive power ever in the history of the
GUY	yes yes
SAM	and now space
GUY	stars
SAM	eternity filled with our
GUY	love you so
SAM	more and more

6.

SAM	faster
GUY	I'm
SAM	threat to our security
GUY	ok
SAM	if anyone harbours
GUY	I'm on it
SAM	retaliate against the facilities of the host country
GUY	yes
SAM	now
GUY	calm
SAM	got to plant bombs in the hotels in Havana
GUY	yes ok ok the Cuban exiles in Miami are just
SAM	and get the money to Iraq
GUY	done it, the Iraqi National Accord have the
SAM	and have they destabilised Saddam yet? no

GUY	car bombs
SAM	giving them millions
GUY	hundred civilians dead
SAM	not enough to
GUY	ok
SAM	fucking results
GUY	off my back will you?
SAM	desperate for
GUY	mujahadeen
SAM	yes yes train the
GUY	so ok that's something really good
SAM	stop at nothing, flaying, explosions, whole villages
GUY	and here we're getting on with assassinations
SAM	don't allow
GUY	changing our
SAM	do allow
GUY	ok
SAM	so get on with
GUY	CIA's Health Alteration Committee
SAM	great
GUY	planning

SAM   Castro, Allende, Ayatollah Khomeini

GUY   Lumumba, Osama, Charles de Gaulle

SAM   Michael Manley

GUY   Ngo Din Diem

SAM   but not all the bastards are dead so

GUY   disappeared, thousands and

SAM   all over the

GUY   impact

SAM   and what what fucking terror used against us

GUY   not my fault they

SAM   fucking Afghanis turned against us after all we

GUY   training camps and now

SAM   stop them

GUY   I'm

SAM   and Israel, innocent

GUY   body parts

SAM   vile

GUY   but the Israelis killing far more so

SAM   on top of this?

GUY   explosion at the embassy

SAM   fuck fuck do something

GUY   stop shouting at me because

SAM   on my side?

GUY   of course but

SAM   want to go home to your

GUY   maybe I do if you're going to keep

SAM   fuck off then back

GUY   look out we're being

SAM   no no no the towers

GUY   wow

SAM   evil

GUY   ok?

SAM   hate me because I'm so good

GUY   all these terrorists suddenly

SAM   makes everyone love me because it's only the evildoers who hate me, you don't hate me

GUY   no of course

SAM   you hate me

GUY   just sometimes wish you'd

SAM   what? what? you hate me

GUY   but maybe I can't live with you any more

7.

SAM *alone.*

SAM   white double cable whip, iron wreath,
beating the soles of the feet, put object in
vagina, put object in anus, put turpentine
on testicles, pour water over face, play
very loud Indonesian music, electric
shocks to genitals, tap a dowl through the
ear into the brain, throw the prisoner out
of the helicopter, show the prisoner
another prisoner being thrown out of the
helicopter, beating obviously, rape of
course, bright light, no sleep, simulate an
execution so they think up to the last
second they're going to die, play tape of
women and children screaming in next
room and tell prisoner it's his wife and
children, sometimes it is, hang up with
hands tied behind back, pins in eyes,
insecticide in hood over the head, cut off
breasts, pull out heart, slit throat and pull
tongue through, sulphuric acid, chop off

Enter GUY.

GUY   hello, I've

SAM   what you

GUY   but I missed you

SAM   same as before

GUY   try and

SAM   what you put me through

GUY   I'm sorry I

SAM   hurt me

GUY   yes I

SAM   take you back I need to know if

GUY   try to

SAM   total commitment or there's no

GUY   I realise

SAM   capable

GUY   can

SAM   promise

GUY   love

SAM   nightmare here

GUY   yes

SAM   not going to be happy, hope you don't

GUY   no I don't expect

SAM   so what you

GUY   can't live

SAM   no you can't, can't

GUY   no I can't

SAM	ok then
GUY	doing?
SAM	need to teach
GUY	yes
SAM	special advisers
GUY	ok
SAM	Greece
GUY	the colonels' Greece, we're right behind
SAM	Operation Phoenix
GUY	Vietnam, operational
SAM	nobody questioned survives
GUY	forty-one thousand
SAM	teaching them in Brazil exactly how much electric shock you can administer without killing
GUY	because sometimes you may not want
SAM	sometimes it's not politic
GUY	and sometimes it just doesn't matter
SAM	El Salvador, Uraguay, Nicaragua, Guatemala,
GUY	delivering the manuals to Panama
SAM	and the thin wire can go in the diplomatic bag to Uraguay
GUY	thin wire?

SAM	against the gum and it increases the shock
GUY	need to be accurate
SAM	precise pain
GUY	for precise effect
SAM	so practice on beggars in a soundproof room
GUY	the US Office of Public Safety
SAM	fighting terror
GUY	put Mitrione in charge of
SAM	humanitarian
GUY	expert in administration of pain
SAM	always leave them some hope, he says
GUY	people who don't need our encouragement because they already
SAM	Afghanistan
GUY	yes the game where the men are on horses and the prisoner
SAM	instead of a goat
GUY	one layer of skin at a time, which must take
SAM	so relatively speaking, Guantanamo
GUY	need results
SAM	need exemption from rules forbidding cruel, inhuman or degrading

GUY	because those rules
SAM	in the present climate
GUY	hoods over their heads or sexual
SAM	because their religion makes them upset by
GUY	menstrual blood
SAM	have to laugh
GUY	but some things we'd rather other people
SAM	747 rendering prisoners to
GUY	because there's plenty of places where that can
SAM	can't do everything ourselves
GUY	do our best
SAM	you're doing great again
GUY	back with you
SAM	no fun though
GUY	sick today but
SAM	just stick with it and we'll be

8.

GUY   icecaps

SAM   who fucking cares about

GUY   floods

SAM   because we'll all be dead by the time it

GUY   another hurricane moving towards

SAM   natural

GUY   no but it's greater than

SAM   natural disasters

GUY   not coping very

SAM   surprise

GUY   predicted and there is an element of manmade

SAM   stop fucking going on about

GUY   carbon

SAM   junk science.

GUY   report here from the

SAM   rewrites

GUY   'serious threat to health'

SAM	delete
GUY	'growing risk of adverse'
SAM	delete
GUY	'uncertainties'
SAM	insert 'significant and fundamental'
GUY	but
SAM	'urgent action,' delete
GUY	oil lobby?
SAM	Committee for a Constructive Tomorrow
GUY	ok
SAM	Advancement of Sound Science Coalition
GUY	a grassroots
SAM	set up by Exxon and Philip Morris to
GUY	ok
SAM	and carbon dioxide in the atmosphere has many beneficial effects on
GUY	hot in here?
SAM	always finding something wrong with
GUY	and you never?
SAM	let's just
GUY	ok
SAM	what? what? you smoking? you gave up, you

GUY	don't care because
SAM	kill yourself
GUY	fucking planet
SAM	kill me, kill me, secondhand
GUY	junk science
SAM	put it out
GUY	no
SAM	put it out
GUY	what difference
SAM	thank you
GUY	carbon
SAM	can't see it in the air, so
GUY	Kyoto?
SAM	price of electricity in California
GUY	but
SAM	nuclear
GUY	waste
SAM	solution
GUY	Iran?
SAM	Technology Institute will come up with new
GUY	by when will they

SAM   if you're so smart

GUY   different

SAM   freedom to

GUY   if

SAM   lose everything we've

GUY   hard to

SAM   things I need

GUY   look out

SAM   what?

GUY   don't know, I thought

SAM   deep breaths and

GUY   don't want to stop flying

SAM   trade in carbon so we can still

GUY   we'll last longer than

SAM   don't let them in

GUY   no water

SAM   be ok

GUY   catastrophe

SAM   so fucking negative

GUY   frightened

SAM   leave me if you don't

GUY   done that

SAM   stay then and be some

GUY   hopeless

SAM   and try to smile

GUY   dead

SAM   because you have to love me

GUY   can't

SAM   love me love me, you have to love me, you

End.